Fast Fashion

Sally Cowan

Contents

Fast Fashion

What Is Fast Fashion?

Fast fashion is cheap, **trendy** clothing that can quickly go out of style. This type of clothing is made in large amounts and comes in many designs so that fast fashion stores always have new clothes for sale. The companies that produce fast fashion use cheap fabrics and quick **manufacturing** methods to keep clothing prices low. These clothes are not made to last for a long time, so the fabrics can soon rip or become **pilled** and unattractive, buttons can fall off or zips can break.

Fast fashion has become popular in the twenty-first century. Many shoppers think it is easy to throw cheap clothes away and buy new ones. They do not want to repair their clothes or spend lots of money buying better-quality clothes that will last longer. Fast fashion companies have encouraged this "throw-away" attitude because they make more money when they sell more clothes.

Fast fashion clothes are thrown away in large amounts and can end up in landfill.

Zips can break easily on fast fashion clothing, making the clothes unusable.

Fast fashion is made in busy clothing factories by using quick manufacturing methods.

Selling Fast Fashion

Fast fashion is sold in stores and on the internet. The companies that sell fast fashion spend lots of money on advertisements to persuade people to buy more clothes.

There are many fast fashion **brands.** Their stores are usually located on city streets and in large shopping centres. The store windows will have attractive displays of the latest styles, and large signs with special offers. Inside the stores, which sometimes take up two or three floors, rows and rows of clothing racks hold a variety of styles. If any clothing is not selling, the price is soon reduced – the store owners need to sell the clothes quickly to make room for new styles.

Fast fashion stores have rows of fashionable clothes for sale.

Shoppers can find even more fashion brands, advice and special offers online, where they can easily buy clothing with just the tap of a finger. The clothes are then delivered to shoppers' homes.

Shoppers can browse for new clothes from their own homes by using the internet.

This is how fast fashion works today, but buying clothes wasn't always like this. So, how did fast fashion come about?

Before Fast Fashion

A Home Handicraft

In the last 250 years, methods of making clothes have sped up. But before then, making clothes was very slow work. It was a **handicraft** that people did at home.

Most people had to produce the natural materials for their clothes themselves. They kept sheep to get wool and grew crops to make other threads, such as cotton and linen. Then they had to **spin** the wool or remove the **fibres** from the plants to turn them into yarn or thread for knitting and weaving. They also prepared leather and fur from animal skins to cut and sew into clothing.

Only royalty and wealthy people could afford fashionable clothing. Most people wore basic clothes for practical reasons: to cover themselves, to keep warm or be protected from the sun, and to look neat and tidy when they went out.

a cotton plant that is ready to be picked and turned into thread

This painting from the 1600s shows a woman and a boy wearing simple clothes, made with thread from a spinning wheel.

Royal fashion from the 1600s was full of rich colours and expensive fabrics.

Making Fabrics with Machines

In the late 1700s, new machines were invented in Great Britain. They could produce fabrics much more quickly than people could at home. These machines were set up in large buildings called factories. This change to using machines to make goods is called the "Industrial Revolution".

One of the first machines made during the Industrial Revolution was the "spinning jenny", which was a mechanical version of a spinning wheel. The spinning jenny had many **spindles** and was used to spin wool and cotton into thread.

The power **loom** was another important machine. It was used for weaving spun threads together to make fabric.

a spinning jenny machine

Many people left their homes to find work in the factories. The workers did repetitive tasks for long hours and low pay. The new machines were not built with the safety of the workers in mind, so accidents were common.

A woman uses a power loom to make fabric in England in the early 1900s.

Fashion Becomes Popular

In the 1800s, the Industrial Revolution spread throughout Europe, the USA and other parts of the world. As factory owners and business people became wealthy, they could afford to pay dressmakers and **tailors** to make their clothing according to fashion trends. At that time, fashion was changing slowly, and people wore their clothes many times.

Meanwhile, factory workers could not afford fashionable clothes. Most workers did not even earn enough money to look after themselves and their families. Parents often had to send their children to work in the factories to add to the family's income.

Young boys work in a cotton factory in Georgia, USA in 1909, performing dangerous jobs by climbing on the machines.

In the mid-1800s, the first sewing machine was invented. Clothes could now be made even more quickly and cheaply. Large **fashion houses** began to sell clothes for two fashion seasons each year: spring/summer and autumn/winter.

Fashion shows and magazines became popular, and more people were interested in fashion. When sewing machines became cheaper, even poor workers could afford them. The workers could then make their own clothes, copying the styles they saw in fashion magazines.

This French magazine from the nineteenth century was published every month with new fashions.

A woman uses an early sewing machine in her home.

Fashion Speeds Up

In the 1930s, another big change sped up how clothes were made. New fibres called **synthetics**, made from chemicals, became popular. The first synthetic fabric was nylon, which looks like expensive silk. It was cheaper to make fabrics from synthetic fibres than natural fibres. Many people liked the clothes made from synthetic fabrics because they were cheap to buy and easy to wash.

From the 1940s onwards, ready-made clothes were sold in shops and large stores, but these clothes were often **conservative**. Fashionable clothing from the fashion houses was expensive, so many people still made their clothes at home.

nylon being made in a factory in Thailand

Hanni Vanhaiden, a German TV presenter, models colourful fashion in 1970.

During the 1960s and 70s, many young people wanted to wear more modern styles of clothing made from colourful synthetic fabrics. More brands were created to produce new fashion trends, such as flared pants and miniskirts. But it would take another 20 years for fast fashion to arrive.

Fast Fashion Arrives

Fast fashion became available in stores in the 1990s. By this time, clothing styles had become more relaxed and varied. New synthetic fabrics, such as fake fur, lace and silk, made it possible to buy expensive-looking clothes at cheap prices.

With the expansion of the internet in the early 2000s, millions of people were able to instantly see the latest fashions online. They did not have to wait for magazines to report the newest trends.

Fashion became a worldwide topic of interest. People were excited to see what their favourite celebrities were wearing during their everyday lives. **Social media** became a way for people to discuss fashion trends and how to achieve the latest "looks" worn by celebrities more cheaply. Online shopping also made it easier for people to buy trendy clothing, no matter where they lived.

A fashion blogger models a trendy outfit during New York Fashion Week in 2018.

Actor Timothée Chalamet wore this “motorcycle” style outfit in 2022, following a new trend from fashion houses.

Today, fast fashion companies continue to make clothing extremely quickly. Their clothing collections are not limited to two fashion seasons a year, now. Some companies can produce new styles in about two weeks, from the illustrated design to the finished item arriving in stores.

Workers and Fast Fashion

Fast fashion has led to the **exploitation** of many workers.

Most fast fashion factories are located in developing countries, such as Bangladesh, Vietnam, Indonesia and China. These countries have a large supply of workers and factories, so clothes can be made quickly and cheaply there.

However, workers are not paid well, and they can get sick from working long hours every day of the week. The chemicals that are used to dye fabrics can also harm the health of workers, and breathing in fabric fibres every day can damage the workers' lungs.

Many of these factories are badly built and unsafe to work in. The factory floors are often crowded with workers, machines and rolls of fabric. Accidents sometimes happen, and it can be difficult for workers to escape if there is a fire.

Clothing workers in Bangladesh protest for better pay and working conditions.

Clothing workers in a factory in China operate sewing machines in cramped conditions.

Fast Fashion and the Environment

Fast fashion can harm the environment in many different ways.

The chemicals used to make dyes and other fabric treatments can leak into rivers, lakes and oceans. They can then poison ecosystems and kill plants, fish and other animals.

Every time a piece of clothing made from synthetic material is washed, tiny fibres or pieces of plastic called **microfibres** break off. The microfibres then flow out through pipes and pollute waterways. Microfibres not only pollute neighbourhood waterways, but water all over the world, from mountain glaciers to the deepest parts of the ocean. The microfibres from natural fabrics can also be harmful if they contain chemicals from dyes and fabric treatments. Sea life swallow or absorb these microfibres, which can make them sick.

Microfibres from clothing have been found far from cities and factories, even inside the sea ice of the Antarctic.

Chemicals and microfibres from fast fashion can pollute marine ecosystems.

Chemicals can pollute rivers, harming fish and plants.

Fast fashion is creating a lot of waste. Every day, people throw unwanted clothing into their rubbish bins. Some people give their clothing to charity shops, but the clothes are often unwearable because of their poor quality. While some clothing is passed to companies that can make them into rags, many clothes are sent to landfill.

Piles of unwanted clothes end up in landfills in Africa, such as this one in Kenya.

Huge amounts of second-hand clothing are shipped to places that are less wealthy, such as countries in Africa. The clothes are sorted and sold in markets, but many clothes are unwearable, so they are thrown into rubbish dumps. Enormous mounds of fast fashion clothing from all over the world are polluting the land and waterways of these countries, because they do not have the resources to deal with the waste.

Only the better-quality items among the second-hand clothing shipped to Africa can be sold in markets.

The End of Fast Fashion?

The problems caused by fast fashion are becoming more well known. Now, many shoppers are thinking carefully about their buying habits and are trying to change them.

The rise of **sustainable** fashion brands has given shoppers an alternative to fast fashion. Sustainable clothing companies pay their workers properly and make sure their workplaces are safe. No harsh dyes or chemical treatments are used to make the clothing, so that workers and the environment are not harmed.

Sustainable clothing companies usually have tags on their clothes to explain where the materials came from.

Sustainable fashion companies have to spend more money producing their clothes, which makes the clothes more expensive to buy. However, supporters of sustainable fashion encourage people to buy less clothing and to make careful choices when they do buy clothes.

Sustainable fashion has fewer styles than fast fashion, but the clothing is of better quality.

Some people are learning to repair their clothes so they can last longer.

Shoppers can find unique items in charity shops.

People are also **reviving** some of the sewing skills that their great-grandparents used. They prefer to repair their clothing, rather than throw it out. Others like to search charity shops for better-quality clothing and unique items that express their personalities.

Today, some of the fast fashion brands are changing, too. Some are using more sustainable materials and choosing not to exploit their workers. If more shoppers change their attitudes and decide to pay more for sustainable clothing, fast fashion may be on the way out.

A store in France advertises that it is a sustainable clothing business.

We Need to Slow Down Fashion

My friends and I think we should all reduce the amount of fast fashion that we buy. Today, a lot of clothes are thrown away because we no longer like them or they need to be repaired. We want to hold a Slow Down Fashion Day at school to repair our clothes and swap unwanted clothes with other students – with our parents' permission, of course! We believe there would be several benefits to having a Slow Down Fashion Day.

First, if we swap or repair clothes instead of throwing them away, we can help to reduce the amount of clothing waste in the world. When clothes are sent to landfill, they get mixed in with other rubbish, including plastics and metals. This stops the clothes from breaking down quickly. Huge piles of clothes could take hundreds of years to break down, and sometimes the fabrics are made with toxic chemicals that pollute the ground. If every student brought just one piece of clothing to Slow Down Fashion Day, it would significantly reduce the amount of rubbish going to our local landfill.

When clothes are sent to landfill, they can cause a lot of damage to the environment.

Second, Slow Down Fashion Day would help change students' attitudes towards clothing. This would save us and our parents from wasting money on low-quality clothes. Just because a button has fallen off, the fabric has ripped or a seam has come apart, it doesn't mean that the clothing is unusable and should be thrown out.

My friends and I have learnt sewing skills in art class this term. We would be very willing to sew on any buttons or make repairs to clothes that need them. We can also show others how to do these repairs. This would encourage students to wear their clothes for longer. They might even get some ideas on how to alter their clothes to make them look unique, for example, by sewing on patches or changing all the buttons.

Colourful patches and stitches can make a piece of clothing fun and different.

Finally, Slow Down Fashion Day would encourage us to clean out our wardrobes. Some of us have wardrobes bursting with clothes that no longer fit, and we don't all have little brothers or sisters to pass our clothing on to. Because children grow out of their clothes quickly, many of these clothes might still be in good condition. Some outfits might only have been worn for special occasions. It would be a thoughtful idea to let other students wear these clothes. Then others could get as much enjoyment from the clothes as the original wearer did.

Passing down clothes that no longer fit to other students can make clothes last longer.

My friends and I want to do all we can to avoid buying fast fashion. We can all help to reduce pollution, as well as learn how to repair our clothes and help other students. We believe a Slow Down Fashion Day at school would be an enormous success!

Glossary

brands (*noun*)	companies that are recognised by their name or logo
conservative (*adjective*)	staying the same, not changing with trends
exploitation (*noun*)	unfair or cruel treatment
fashion houses (*noun*)	companies that design and produce expensive and beautiful clothes
fibres (*noun*)	small, thin threads that make up materials such as wool or cotton
handicraft (*noun*)	work that is done by hand to make an object
loom (*noun*)	a frame used for weaving thread
manufacturing (*noun*)	the process of making a product, usually with machines in factories
microfibres (*noun*)	tiny pieces that break off fabrics
pilled (*adjective*)	when little balls of fluff have formed on the surface of a fabric
reviving (*verb*)	bringing back something that has not been done for a while
social media (*noun*)	websites and apps that allow users to create and share content with other users
spin (*verb*)	to twist and pull fibres to make thread

spindles (*noun*) thin rods that thread is wound onto

sustainable (*adjective*) using materials and methods to make sure a resource is available in the future

synthetics (*noun*) fabrics that are made from chemicals rather than natural materials

tailors (*noun*) people who make clothes to perfectly fit individual people

trendy (*adjective*) new and popular

Index